IT'S MY STATE! ★

NEBRASKA

Doug Sanders

 Cavendish Square

New York

Published in 2014 by Cavendish Square Publishing, LLC
303 Park Avenue South, Suite 1247, New York, NY 10010

Library of Congress Cataloging-in-Publication Data

Sanders, Doug, 1972-
Nebraska / Doug Sanders.
     pages cm. — (It's my state)
Includes index.
 ISBN 978-1-62712-241-2 (hardcover) ISBN 978-1-62712-498-0 (paperback) ISBN 978-1-62712-252-8 (ebook)
1. Nebraska—Juvenile literature. I. Title.

 F666.3.S26 2014
 978.2—dc23

            2013034180

This edition developed for Cavendish Square Publishing by RJF Publishing LLC (www.RJFpublishing.com)
Series Designer, Second Edition: Tammy West/Westgraphix LLC
Editorial Director: Dean Miller
Editor: Sara Howell
Copy Editor: Cynthia Roby
Art Director: Jeffrey Talbot
Layout Design: Erica Clendening
Production Manager: Jennifer Ryder-Talbot

CONTENTS

State Flower: Goldenrod

Several species, or types, of the state flower thrive in the soils of Nebraska. In the 1800s, Ida Brockman, daughter of a state lawmaker, wrote an article in support of the flower, saying "It is native, and only a true native should be our representative. It has a long season, and nothing could better represent the hardy endurance of Nebraska's pioneers." The goldenrod was declared the state flower in 1895.

State Bird: Western Meadowlark

The western meadowlark was officially adopted as the state bird in 1929. This symbol of the plains is known for the bubbling tones of its gentle song. Well adapted to prairie life, these birds nest on the ground in secluded areas in fields and meadows.

State Tree: Cottonwood

Hundreds of years ago, when present-day Nebraska was still a territory, cottonwoods served as important landmarks for pioneers heading west. In 1937 the American elm was first chosen as the state tree. Then in 1972 the state legislature selected the cottonwood. A tough tree associated with the pioneer spirit, cottonwoods can be found throughout the state.

State Mammal: White-tailed Deer

In 1981 the state legislature named the white-tailed deer the official state mammal. These plant eaters are a common sight in the forests, meadows, and cornfields of the state. Males have antlers that they shed in the winter and grow again in early spring. Females typically give birth to one or two fawns. The babies usually have white spots on their fur, which disappear by the time the fawn is one year old.

State Fish: Channel Catfish

This popular sport fish can weigh up to 60 pounds (27.2 kg). It gets its cat-related name from the eight "whiskers" growing from its chin. These are actually barbels covered in taste buds. You can identify channel catfish by their narrow heads, forked tails, and rounded fins. Channel catfish are commonly found along the gravelly bottoms of streams and lakes. The channel catfish was named the state fish in 1997.

State Gemstone: Blue Agate

Blue agate, also called blue chalcedony, was declared the state's official gemstone in 1967. It is often found in northwestern Nebraska and can be used to make jewelry. Although it is often blue in color, it has been found in other colors as well.

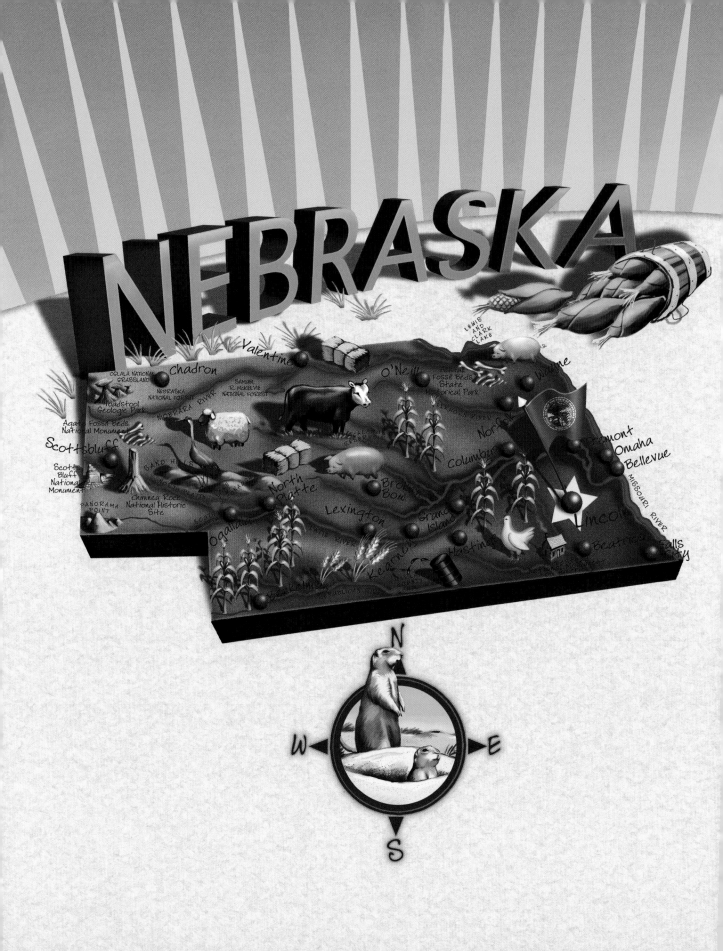

The Cornhusker State

The landscape of Nebraska is as varied as its people. Stately towers of rock jut into the sky, like lookouts stationed above the rolling prairie below. Shallow rivers and streams drift across the state. Many are bordered by cliff-like formations called buttes. Much of the land surface of the state is marked by gentle, sloping plains. The land gently increases in elevation as the state spreads to the west.

One word that could be used to describe Nebraska is timeless. Rambling across the state, it is possible to imagine the Native Americans who once hunted the plains or the long trains of prairie schooners, or covered wagons, that slowly rolled their way west. The state's forested bluffs and tallgrass prairies have changed little from the time these first settlers entered the state.

Still, Nebraska has seen many changes. What military explorer Stephen Long called the "Great Desert" in 1820 is now dotted with manmade lakes and reservoirs. Suburbs and cities have come to a land where once the only skyscraper was the spire of Chimney Rock piercing the horizon in the western part of the state.

Quick Facts

Nebraska's Borders

North	South Dakota
South	Kansas
Southwest	Colorado
East	Iowa
	Missouri
West	Wyoming

It is the state's balance of close-knit communities and wide-open spaces, of the timeless landscape and the modern world that many Nebraskans find so appealing. From rushing rivers and vast prairies to the wild moonscapes that mark parts of its panhandle, Nebraska has it all. As one resident of Chadron noted, "It's America's best-kept secret."

Eastern Nebraska

The Missouri River forms the entire eastern border of the state. It runs along part of the state's northern border as well. Nebraska is the only state located entirely within that great river's basin. "Big Muddy," as the Missouri River is often called, is a lifeline to the region, a major waterway known for its rich history and varied beauty. Lined in places by chalkstone bluffs, the river's many islands and sandbars serve as reminders of the challenges early riverboat captains faced as they chugged along the gentle waters.

Gentle valleys and rolling hills mark this part of the state. The crests, or tops, of these often steep hills are generally rounded, worn down by years of erosion. The hills are partly made up of what is called glacial till. Millions of years ago,

The Missouri River winds its way across the state. Near Decatur, it reaches an average depth of around 20 feet (6 m).

Ancient bones can be found at the Ashfall Fossil Beds State Historical Park in northeastern Nebraska. The remains of birds, turtles, horses, camels, rhinos, wild dogs, deer, and even the seeds of trees and grasses have been found there.

massive glaciers had spread into the heart of the North American continent. As the climate changed and the last Ice Age ended, these giant sheets of ice slowly retreated north. Along the way, they tilled, or churned and ground up, the soil beneath. What was left behind was a deep and rich layer known as till. Later, dirt and dust carried by the wind (and known as loess) added another layer to the Nebraskan landscape. Loess makes up the eastern third of the state, including the region south of the Platte River. Over the years, rivers and streams cut their way through the region, giving the land the look it bears today.

Today this part of the state is marked by farms and communities. More than four-fifths of Nebraska's population live in this part of the state. Omaha, the state's largest city, is found there as well. With its blend of big-city life and laid-back small-town atmosphere, many find it an ideal setting. Others prefer

Lincoln, the state's capital, located less than an hour to the southwest of Omaha. This university town draws students from across the country and around the world.

The Great Plains

For many, when they think of Nebraska, the first image that comes to mind is the Great Plains. Stretching westward, nearly three-quarters of the state is covered by the prairies and grasslands that make up the Great Plains and mark the American heartland. This plains region stretches beyond the state line into neighboring Wyoming and Colorado.

Included in this area are the High Plains, reaching into north-central and western Nebraska. With its towering rock formations, steep buttes, eroded hills, and deep canyons, this part of Nebraska offers some of the state's most unusual sights. The western stretch of the High Plains contains its own share of rugged beauty. Blanketed in evergreen trees, Wildcat Hills and Pine Ridge offer some of the state's most memorable scenery.

Nebraska is known for its practically treeless plains. Early settlers used sod—blocks of earth and grass roots—to build their simple shelters in the early days of the territory.

A region of the state known as the Nebraska Everglades reveals yet another unique natural feature found in the Cornhusker State. The area borders two major rivers and several lakes. Marshy patches and stretches of open water show the curious traveler that Nebraska is much more than a flat, grassy plain.

From its southeastern corner to the High Plains of the west, the state slowly gains elevation. Near the border with Wyoming, the land is more than 1 mile (1.6 km) above sea level. So it is not surprising that the area is home to the state's highest point. Found in Kimball County in the southwestern tip of the Panhandle, Panorama Point reaches 5,426 feet (1,654 m) above sea level.

Loess covers the central and southern plains. The landscape here is not as flat as many believe. Rolling hills break up the flatter, wide-open spaces. In south-central Nebraska is a heavily farmed part of the prairie called the Loess Plains. Flat and regular, it covers roughly 7,000 square miles (18,130 sq km).

In general the plains receive little rain, which often poses a threat to farmers. Nebraska's farmers have led the way in developing systems of irrigation that help them make a living out of the land. Nebraskans are currently the largest producers and users of center-pivot irrigation. This system allows more water to be spread over a larger area with less waste. However, new research is showing that center-pivot irrigation may be damaging to underground aquifers.

The Sandhills

Covering most of north-central Nebraska is one of the state's most unique regions. The Sandhills are the largest stable sand-dune groupings in the Northern Hemisphere. Still considered a part of the Great Plains, the Nebraska Sandhills were probably blown in from the west, first forming nearly 10,000 years ago. When Zebulon Pike passed through the region, he wrote: "this area may in time become as famous as the deserts of Africa." While his prediction did not come entirely true, it is still a unique region nonetheless.

The Sandhills cover about 20,000 square miles (51,800 sq km), or one-fourth of the state. The surrounding region is dotted with various marshes and lakes. This is Nebraska's cattle country. The area's wealth of water—in the form of streams and wells—and rich supply of grass have helped ranching to thrive.

The wind has played a major role in shaping this part of the state. It has shifted and piled billions of grains of sand to form the ridges and hills that seem to fold back onto themselves. Some consider Sandhills the wrong name for the region, as there is little sand in sight. Instead, tall and short grasses grow on a thin layer of soil covering the dunes. The grasses filled in and helped to bind the surface of the Sandhills, holding them in place.

Once a rip or crack is opened in this fragile surface, though, the contents underneath begin to spill out. The sand is lifted and carried by the wind, and soon a deep dent is left in the earth. These are called blowouts. They are usually patched by placing layers of old tires or even entire old cars in the holes. This makes the area around the blowout more stable and encourages the grass to return, repairing and resealing the holes.

The Panhandle

The Panhandle is home to some of the state's most striking features. Toadstool Geologic Park marks a part of the state commonly called the Badlands. Here, the land buckles and folds, twisting and turning into a vast array of unusual shapes. The "toadstools," or mushrooms, found in the park are actually slabs of sandstone perched on top of "stems" made of brule clay. These strange formations were sculpted by wind and water over thousands of years. The soft clay bases eroded more quickly than their sandstone caps and thus suggested the shape of giant mushrooms. Eventually the toadstools collapse under the weight of the sandstone. However, new ones continue to form to replace them.

The Sandhills are a fascinating part of the state. The region—which is the largest stable sand-dune grouping in the Northern Hemisphere—resembles a desert covered in grass or a sea of gently bobbing dunes.

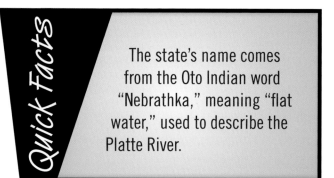
With its wealth of fossils, the park also offers a window into what life was like in the heart of the continent between 38 and 24 million years ago. Still visible on some of the rocks are the preserved tracks of ancient animals that passed through the region. Hugging the southern part of the Panhandle are two impressive landmarks. Chimney Rock stands like a beacon above the plains and can be seen from great distances away. It stretches 500 feet (152 m) above the Platte River and is made of brule clay, volcanic ash, and Arickaree sandstone.

Scotts Bluff is another unexpected sight, rising out of the prairie. A huge plateau, it towers 800 feet (244 m) above the land. The peak can be reached on foot or by car and offers sweeping views of the countryside for more than 100 miles (161 km) in all directions. These two unique features became well known to the

Scotts Bluff was an important landmark on the Oregon Trail. It was designated as a national monument in 1919.

pioneers making their way across the plains along the Oregon Trail. Like prairie signposts, they marked the end of roughly one-third of the journey from Kansas City to the West Coast.

Also found in the Panhandle is one of the nation's richest fossil beds. Preserved so it can be studied and enjoyed by countless generations, Agate Fossil Beds National Monument allows visitors to peer deep into the ancient past. The park contains the fossil evidence of the wealth of mammals that lived in the region during the Miocene period, 20 million years

Years of wind and water have shaped the sandstone slabs found in Toadstool Geologic Park in the state's panhandle. Visitors are encouraged to ramble through the park's bizarre shapes.

ago. Clearly Nebraska was a much different place then. Small, two-horned rhinoceroses, 10-foot-(3 m) long predator pigs, and a mammal—described as a combination of a horse, giraffe, tapir, and a bear—roamed the grasslands.

Among the most unusual finds at the site are the preserved burrows of a land beaver called Paleocastor. Like today's prairie dogs, these large rodents lived together in dens tucked deep beneath the surface of the plains. They created spiral-shaped burrows that spun around and around deep in the ancient riverbanks. Early discoverers of the twisting chutes were baffled, calling them

Settlers heading west by covered wagon and on foot could see Chimney Rock getting slowly larger and closer as they approached it from the east.

Daemonelix, or "devil's corkscrews." Scientists believe the unique structures may have been used to confuse and stop curious predators that entered the burrows in search of a meal.

Climate

In a state where farming is so important, climate and weather can be major concerns. A period with little or no rain, called a drought, can be devastating. While southeastern Nebraska can receive up to 30 inches (76.2 cm) of rain and other precipitation each year, the Panhandle is much drier, with averages totaling 17 inches (43 cm) per year. In recent years, droughts affecting the state have ranged from mild to severe. There is little that can be done to control the weather, though. To show how important the subject is, the state has set up two agencies to focus on weather issues and concerns. The Climate Assessment and Response Committee and the Nebraska State Climate Office study weather trends and provide forecasts and advice in dealing with the often harsh conditions.

Nebraska has a mild climate. Warm summers, cold but not-too-snowy winters, lots of sunshine, and average humidity are the rule. Nonetheless, state residents have learned to adjust to the occasional seasonal extremes. Nebraskans

A tornado can spell disaster to a Nebraska farmer. This one spins and snakes its way across the fields outside Stuart.

also know that the expected can turn into the unexpected in a flash. Early evening thunderstorms are a common event in the summertime, especially in the eastern and central portions of the state. The sky blackens and thick masses of clouds churn in the sky. Nebraska is located squarely in the line of what is called America's Tornado Alley. Nebraskans know that, at certain times, when storms arrive, it is best to run for cover. Many tornados have ripped across the state, causing terrible damage and threatening lives.

Storm chasers, people who follow and study tornados and other dramatic weather events, find Nebraska a prime hunting ground for violent weather. A team of these curious thrill-seekers travels throughout the Midwest in the spring and summer. They drive special storm-chasing vehicles, equipped with Doppler radar and other devices that allow them to collect data and to track and study storms. Another storm-chasing tool is the tornado-intercept vehicle. These armored vehicles are equipped with IMAX cameras and allow film crews to drive inside the swirling and dangerous storm systems.

Wildlife

Although forests cover only two percent of the state, Nebraska still has its share of trees. Oaks, elms, box elders, basswood, ash, and hackberry are just a few of the trees that can be seen wafting in the prairie winds. One of the state's major wooded areas can be found along the Niobrara River valley. It took root in the moist, rich soil and spread from the east, almost halfway across the state. To the northwest, the rugged Pine Ridge region is another trove of tree life. As its name implies, it is an area known for its impressive stands of pine.

Perhaps the state's most impressive forest, though, is the product of its hardworking residents. The first US Forest Service nursery in the country is the Nebraska State Forest. Located near Halsey, it is the world's largest woodland planted entirely by hand. The forest was originally created to draw potential settlers to the otherwise barren region. Few settlers came, but the trees helped curb erosion and prevent the dusty topsoil from being carried away by the wind.

The most common form of plant life in the Cornhusker State is the wealth of native prairie grasses for which the state is known. These varied species house, hide, and feed an equally impressive array of animal life. Mule deer, white-tailed deer, pronghorn antelope, bison, elk, and bighorn sheep are just a few of the four-footed creatures that make the state their home. Coyotes and bobcats pad across the prairie in search of food, while along the state's rivers and streams, beavers, muskrats, and mink thrive. Raccoons are drawn to the water as well to try their hand at fishing. Trout, perch, bass, catfish, carp, pike, and crappies abound beneath the surface of the state's many waterways.

With so many crane-watchers descending on the state each year, it is clear that Nebraska is a bird-watcher's paradise. Dedicated birders also enjoy the mating calls and elaborate dances of the sharp-tailed grouse. Pheasants, quail, ducks, snow geese, turkey vultures, whip-poor-wills, great horned owls, and wild turkeys are among the species found in the state. Golden eagles and prairie falcons soar over the grasslands, their sharp eyes searching for rodents and prairie dogs below. Cliff swallows also make an annual appearance in Nebraska. They fly more than 3,000 miles (4,828 km) from Argentina to nest in the state's lake-filled southwestern corner.

The tree-lined Niobrara River swells and surges as it makes its way across northern Nebraska.

Endangered

With so many natural treasures, Nebraskans have made strong efforts to protect the land and the life it supports. The state currently has 15 species of plants and animals on its list of endangered species. Programs and agencies have been created to make sure the list does not grow. Black-footed ferrets, for example, once roamed the plains freely. With the arrival of settlers from the east, their populations, along with those of several other animals, went down. Today, there have been reports of black-footed ferrets in the wild, but there are no known populations in the state.

Sometimes the best conservation plans help to protect animals long before a species is threatened or endangered. Every year, more and more visitors flock to the 80-mile-(129 km) stretch of the Platte River to witness the annual migration of more than 500,000 cranes. The birds have become a popular attraction each March, as they stop along the river to rest and feed before flying on to their breeding grounds in Canada, Alaska, and parts of Siberia. About 80 percent of the world's population of sandhill cranes passes through the region every year.

The increased tourism has helped the economy of this part of the state. Still, many local residents, biologists, and officials have realized that this economic success must not come at a cost to the birds. While the birds have been traveling to the area for thousands of years, if their habitat is harmed or threatened, or if they feel the pressure of too many people, they may choose another location to stop over on their annual migration.

Two recent million-dollar projects have taken great strides in ensuring the safety and future of Nebraska's beloved seasonal visitors. The Crane Meadows Nature Center, located outside Wood River, offers three

Quick Facts

Nebraska's endangered species list includes three types of birds, two mammals, four types of fish, two insects, one type of mussel, and three types of plants.

blinds—or enclosed shelters—to morning and evening visitors. To the west, the National Audubon Society's Lillian Annette Rowe Bird Sanctuary in Gibbon offers bird-watchers four blinds. The famed nature magazine *National Geographic* has also set up a live, online video feed of the cranes for those who cannot make it to the site in person.

The birds have become popular tourist attractions, each year drawing more and more people from across Nebraska and around the world. With these two new centers, humans and cranes now have the ideal settings in which to coexist. Wildlife centers such as these show that Nebraskans wish to provide a safe, welcoming place for all its visitors, whether they be animal or human.

A majestic symbol of the state, sandhill cranes gather in the shallow waters of the Platte River near Kearney.

Prairie Rattlesnake

The prairie rattler is one of only four species of poisonous snakes living in Nebraska. They are usually found in the western two-thirds of the state on the plains and grasslands. Mostly active in the daytime, these reptiles live off a diet of rabbits, prairie dogs, kangaroo rats, mice, and lizards.

Coyote

The coyote is a relative of the wolf. These highly intelligent animals are mostly active at night, when their sharp barks and howling can be heard drifting across the plains. Coyotes eat birds, insects, dead animals, rodents, and rabbits. They have also been known to stray onto farmers' and ranchers' lands to prey on small livestock.

Pronghorn Antelope

Most of Nebraska's pronghorns are found in the western Panhandle, but smaller populations are located in the Sandhills and central areas of the state as well. Drought and the spread of farms have affected the antelope population. Officials are confident, though, that these nimble mammals—known for their great speed and powerful eyesight—will continue to thrive in the Cornhusker State.

Prairie Chicken

These peculiar birds were once an important food source for Native Americans and settlers living on the plains. Through the years, though, the prairie chickens' range and numbers have greatly decreased. Today a small but growing population makes its home mostly in the central and southeastern portions of Nebraska.

Little Bluestem

Also known as bunch grass or beard grass, little bluestem is found across the Great Plains. It commonly grows in clumps of up to 300 reddish purple stems, which turn a golden color as the plant ages. Little bluestem can reach only a few inches (cm) in height in poor soil or up to 3 feet (0.9 m) in the moister parts of the plains.

Sandhill Crane

These powerful fliers mate for life and can live up to 25 years. Sandhill cranes have been stopping over in Nebraska during their annual migrations for thousands of years. More than half a million birds gather each spring along the Platte River before heading to their summer breeding grounds.

From the Beginning

Humans first entered the central plains around 12,000 years ago, near the end of the last Ice Age. They were mostly hunters, following roving herds of big game. These people, often called the Paleo-Indians, were the ancestors of the Native Americans who would eventually spread across the state. Over thousands of years, these ancient peoples lived on the grasslands that would become the future state of Nebraska. Slowly, weather and climate patterns shifted and became more stable. This, as well as the extinction of several prehistoric species such as the mammoth, encouraged the creation of more permanent settlements. The Paleo-Indians continued hunting and gathering, but eventually started to farm plots of land in and near their villages.

By 2,000 years ago, more complex communities dotted the plains. These early residents made helpful, everyday items out of pottery. They also fished in Nebraska's many rivers and grew to rely more heavily on agriculture. Nebraska was a harsh region to conquer. Periods of drought forced some groups to pack up and search for a better life elsewhere. During times of prosperity, many sought out the future state. The region quickly became a crossroads of Native American life. Even in its earliest days, the state was a lively and diverse mixture of various native languages and culture groups.

Immigrants and pioneers slowly tamed the plains that would form the future state of Nebraska. This family settled in the Loup Valley in 1886.

Native Nebraska

The region that was to become Nebraska was settled by several mighty Native American nations. They came to dominate the central plains well into the 1830s. The Pawnee, and their northern relatives the Arikaras, left perhaps the deepest mark on the region. They first arrived in Nebraska from the south and were well established there by the mid-1500s. They built earthen lodges made of stacked poles covered with brush and packed with mud. These striking structures were a common sight, grouped into villages huddled along the banks of the Platte, Loup, and Republican rivers, to name a few.

Other groups left their mark as well. The Cheyenne, Arapaho, and Lakota (Teton Sioux) pushed west after originally settling in the forests north and east of the Missouri River. The Omaha, Ponca, and Oto were also transplants to the area. They entered the eastern portion of the state in the 1700s and lived in the Missouri River basin as well. By the start of the 1800s, about 40,000 Native Americans called Nebraska home.

This photo from 1871 shows a Pawnee family outside of their earthen lodge near Loup.

George Catlin produced this image of Big Elk, an Omaha warrior, in 1832. The Omaha had originally come from the East and eventually settled in the regions that now include Nebraska and South Dakota.

The arrival of European explorers and settlers changed the Native Americans' lives forever. The introduction of the horse meant they could travel and hunt more effectively. New diseases such as measles and smallpox swept through entire villages, leaving very few standing. Eventually the valuable land the Native Americans held was too tempting to arriving settlers, and the native people were slowly driven from the land. Treaties were made. However, not all the land deals between the US government and the various native nations had been made final by the 1850s when the area became a territory that was suddenly opened for settlement.

MAKING A BANDBOX

In the 1800s people traveling to Nebraska—and to other parts of the country—used bandboxes to carry small objects like gloves and jewelry. The first bandboxes were made by shirt manufacturers to ship men's stiff shirt collars (these collars were called bands).

People found the boxes useful for storage as well as travel. They lined the inside of the box with newspaper and decorated the outside with colorful paper. Following these instructions you can make your own bandbox.

WHAT YOU NEED:

Several sheets of newspaper

An empty round oatmeal container or a similar container

Tape measure and ruler

Pencil

Heavy gift wrapping paper or other colorful paper, about 36 inches (91 cm) long by 36 inches (91 cm) wide

Scissors

Craft glue

Small part of a sponge

Piece of ribbon about 20 inches (51 cm) long and 1 inch (2.5 cm) wide

Spread the newspaper on your work surface and place the wrapping paper on it, design-side down. Use the tape measure to measure the height of the container and the distance around it. Add 1 inch (2.5 cm) to the distance around the container. Now mark your height and distance measurements on the wrapping paper and cut it out.

Have an adult help you with these next steps. Spread glue on the back of the wrapping paper piece. Use a damp sponge to spread the glue thinly and evenly. Center the container on the glue-covered paper. Make sure that the top and bottom edges of the paper are lined up with the top and bottom edges of the container. Carefully roll the container across the paper, making sure the paper sticks to the container. Smooth out any air bubbles that form between the paper and the container.

To decorate the lid, lay some of the remaining wrapping paper on your work surface design-side down. Place the lid on the paper and trace around the circle with a pencil. Cut out the circle, spread glue, and stick the paper to the lid. Use small strips of the wrapping paper to cover the edges of the lid.

Glue the middle of the ribbon to the bottom of your container. (The ribbon should be about 2 1/2 times the height of the container.) Run the ribbon up the sides of the bandbox, using drops of glue to keep it in place. The ribbon should stretch beyond the ends of the container. When the lid is on the bandbox, you can bring the ribbons over the top and tie a bow to keep the box closed. When the glue is dry your bandbox is ready. You can use it to store things or you can use it when giving gifts.

The First Europeans

The first European to make an appearance in the region was Francisco Vásquez de Coronado. He and a crew of men trekked across the American Southwest in 1541, making it all the way to Kansas. The explorer claimed the entire region for Spain.

Coming from a different direction, French explorer Sieur de La Salle sailed down the Mississippi River in 1682. Though he did not set foot in the future state, he claimed all the land drained by the river for King Louis XIV, the ruler of France. This was just the first step in opening the region to curious Europeans seeking their fortune along the American frontier. During the 1690s and early 1700s, trappers and traders crisscrossed the region. By 1714 the French explorer Étienne Veniard de Bourgmont had followed the course of the Missouri River all the way to the mouth of the Platte River.

With competing claims on the continent, Spain and France became rivals for power and control of the New World. The Nebraska region became one source of the conflict. Feeling the French had overstepped their bounds, Spaniard Pedro de Villasur led a group of forty-five men into the area in 1720 with the hopes of expelling, or removing, the French. Before they could do so, though, the group was attacked by Pawnee warriors near the Platte River. In the battle that followed, most of the Spaniards were killed. The French remained in the region, holding tightly to their foothold in Nebraska.

In simple canoes and on foot, the region's first explorers slowly mapped the lands that would form the future state.

In 1739, French explorers Paul and Pierre Mallet, joined by six others, left Illinois in the hope of reaching present-day Santa Fe, New Mexico. Along the way they crossed almost the entire length of Nebraska. They also named the Platte River. Slowly the territory that was to become Nebraska was being mapped and tamed. Events in Europe would cause the region to change hands several times. In 1763, after a costly war in Europe, France gave up all of its land claims west of the Mississippi River to Spain. Like before, though, French fur traders were still working in the now Spanish-controlled region.

For the time being, they were wise in staying. In 1800, French leader Napoléon Bonaparte forced the Spanish to return the land. French control was to be short-lived, though. Three years later, in need of funds, Bonaparte sold the large territory, a deal referred to as the Louisiana Purchase, to the US government.

Napoléon Bonaparte had hoped to build an empire in North America. When that did not seem likely, he sold the Louisiana Territory to the United States for $15 million.

The Americans Arrive

With so much newly acquired land, the Americans were eager to explore their recent purchase. Meriwether Lewis and William Clark and their Corps of Discovery spent three months in the state, starting in 1804. They traveled up the Missouri River and explored what are now the eastern and northern borders of Nebraska. Then, in 1806, Zebulon Pike, on a similar mission, entered and explored south-central Nebraska.

It was not long before trading posts sprang up in the Missouri River valley. The Spanish-American trader Manuel Lisa established a

In Their Own Words

. . . a barren and uncongenial [unpleasant] district

—Major Stephen Long's first impression of Nebraska

This log cabin at Fort Atkinson State Historical Park bears witness to the state's earliest days, when non-native communities were first forming.

string of them from 1807 to 1820. Fort Lisa, one of the posts, was located 10 miles (16 km) from present-day Omaha. The economy of this once-remote region was developing slowly. Trappers and traders, looking to cash in on the wealth of furs they could find to the west, continued to pass through the region. In 1812 fur agent Robert Stuart left Astoria in the Oregon Territory and headed for New York City. Entering Nebraska in 1813, Stuart and his seven companions followed the course of the North Platte River to the point where it joins the South Platte. They then continued along, following the river until it met up with the Missouri River. It would prove to be an ideal path to follow and the future course of the Oregon Trail, which brought countless pioneers deep into the American West.

In 1819 the US Army arrived to build Nebraska's first military post, Fort Atkinson. It was established near the present-day town of Fort Calhoun, located in Washington County. Intended to protect the American frontier, the site became, along with the village of Bellevue, one of the largest communities in Nebraska at the time. With more than 1,000 residents, Fort Atkinson set up the state's first school, library, and grist mill. The fort was eventually abandoned in 1827.

A year after the army arrived, Major Stephen Long and a group of twenty men followed the South Platte to its source near present-day Denver, Colorado. Major Long's now-famous reports talk of a barren and harsh land, unfit for humans. He held little hope that the region would one day prosper. On the simple map that a member of Long's expedition drew, the major had this area, which includes present-day Nebraska, labeled the "Great Desert."

Luckily, Major Long's impressions were wrong. Nebraska would become a thriving territory in no time. Missionaries appeared, including the famed Catholic priest Father Pierre-Jean de Smet, who was eager to work with the Nebraska and Pawnee Native Americans. Fur traders continued to come and go, spreading through the region. They especially flocked to the Platte River route, which quickly grew in popularity. In little more than two decades, Long's great desert would become flooded with thousands of pioneers, eager for a better life in the American West.

The Territory Grows

As more and more American settlers searched for their fortunes in the West, Nebraska became an important center of activity. Both the Oregon Trail and the Mormon Trail wound their way through the region. Pony Express riders followed the well-worn routes that traveled through the Platte River valley. Before the arrival of the railroad, steamboats were important to the trade and transportation of the region.

With so much increased traffic, Fort Kearny was built to offer added protection for the hopeful pioneers headed west. Though white settlers flooded the area, most were only passing through.

By the 1840s, though, Nebraska was on the road to statehood. Secretary of War William Wilkins, in a report from 1844, stated "The Platte or Nebraska River being the central stream would very properly furnish a name to the territory." It was in that year that the first attempt was made to make the area a territory. The measure failed to pass, though. Another bill, known as the Kansas-Nebraska Act, was eventually approved in 1854 after much debate and disagreement. It officially created the Kansas and Nebraska territories and allowed the citizens to decide whether or not slavery would be allowed. Most Nebraskans were against the practice.

The two new regions were created in the hope of increasing settlement west of the Missouri River. Originally the Nebraska Territory was much larger than the state is today. In addition to Nebraska, it included parts of the present-day states of Montana, Wyoming, Colorado, and North and South Dakota. By 1863 the territory had been divided further, leaving Nebraska close to the size and shape it is today.

Cottonwoods still stand at the site of Fort Kearny, though the actual buildings were taken down in 1871.

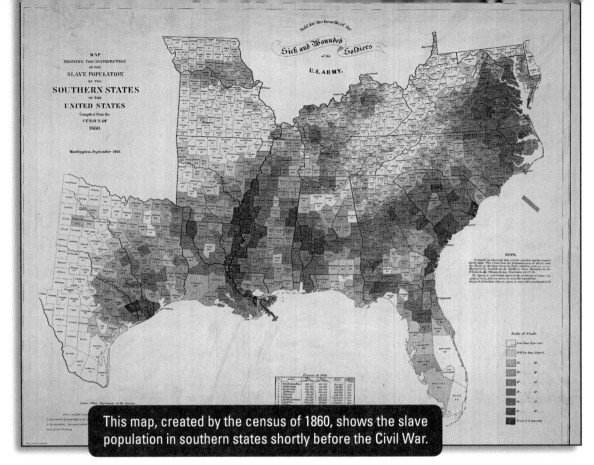

This map, created by the census of 1860, shows the slave population in southern states shortly before the Civil War.

By the 1850s, the nation was deeply divided over the issue of slavery. Those opposed to the practice were worried that the new territories would allow slavery. Those in favor of slavery believed there was no question whether or not it would be allowed in the newly created lands. Both sides clashed and minor conflicts were fought in the region long before the first cannons of the Civil War were fired. (The slavery issue was one of the main reasons for the Civil War.) Slaves were first bought and sold in Nebraska in the 1850s in Nebraska City.

Slavery was not the only issue dividing the newly created territory. Residents and officials disagreed over how the territory would be settled, the creation of new laws, the coming of the railroad, and, most notably, the location of the territorial capital. In addition, there were often regional rivalries between those living north of the Platte River and those who had settled to the south. Many issues remained to be worked out, and the territory was denied statehood when it first attempted to join the Union. Still, the area prospered. From 1854 to 1860, Nebraska's population grew from 2,732 to 28,841.

The Civil War and Beyond

During the Civil War, which began in 1861, the residents of the Nebraska Territory generally supported the Union, or Northern, forces. Volunteers helped form the First Nebraska Infantry under the command of Colonel John M. Thayer. Although disagreement still ran deep among many Nebraskans, the battles never entered the territory and affected the region less than the states located farther to the east.

The passage of the Homestead Act in 1862 increased the territory's population all the more. It granted settlers 160 acres (65 ha) of free western land if they agreed to live and work on it. More hopeful pioneers came to try their hand at working the Nebraska countryside. The major event of the decade was the coming of the Union Pacific Railroad. A line extending westward from Omaha was started in 1865. It reached the western border of the territory two years later. Throughout the 1870s and 1880s, the railroads were big business in the state and did much to change life in the region. To spur the growth and number of railroad lines and to further connect the growing country, the US government

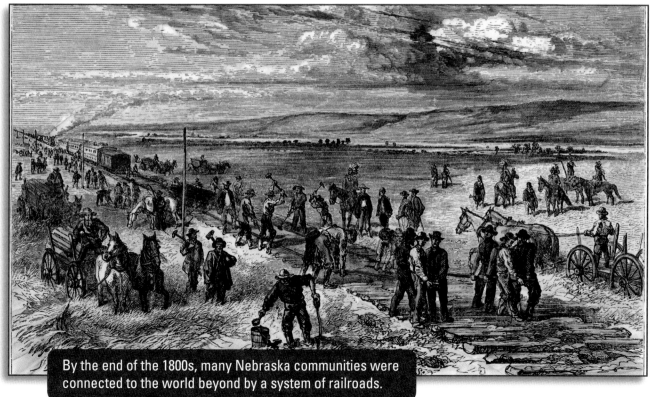

By the end of the 1800s, many Nebraska communities were connected to the world beyond by a system of railroads.

offered certain companies portions of the territory in the form of land grants.

To raise funds in order to build the rail lines, the companies in turn sold large tracts of the land to interested settlers. They often created elaborate ad campaigns to lure new arrivals not only from the East Coast but from Europe as well. The ad campaigns worked. Along with a flood of former Civil War soldiers who also arrived in the region in search of land, the population of Nebraska ballooned to almost 123,000 by 1870. By the mid-1880s the Burlington Railroad lines also crossed the state. Once-remote areas now found themselves in greater contact with the world beyond.

Statehood

Nebraska was finally admitted to the Union on March 1, 1867, but again, not without conflict. The president serving at the time, Andrew Johnson, was a Democrat and did not want the mostly Republican territory to be offered statehood. He vetoed, or rejected, the act of Congress making Nebraska a state. Congress was able to override Johnson's veto. However, lawmakers set down their own terms the territory had to meet before it was allowed into the Union. The Nebraska legislature had to remove a phrase from its proposed state constitution that gave only free white men the right to vote.

The early years of statehood were rough on Nebraska. It was a pattern that had become all too familiar. As was the case with some of Nebraska's early native cultures, the harsh conditions of life on the prairie proved too challenging for some residents. When swarms of grasshoppers descended on the state and destroyed crops, many farm families packed up and headed back east. The state's economy did not surge in the 1870s, and recovery was slow in coming.

With few trees to supply building materials, resourceful residents built their homes from thick blocks of sod. This family settled in Custer County in the 1880s.

By the 1880s, though, the tide had turned. Another large wave of settlers came to the state. New residents, eager for their own homesteads, arrived on the plains. Land prices increased steadily throughout the decade. Once again, however, with the arrival of the 1890s, the state faced hard times. Drought settled on the land, and real estate prices dropped. Many farmers found themselves bankrupt.

Many people called out for change. Farmers felt banks and railroads were concerned only with their own profits. Families and other small operations could not afford the high prices the railroads charged to ship crops and other farm products. Hundreds of Nebraska farmers turned to a new organization called the Farmers' Alliance. It worked to reduce shipping costs and curb the power of large companies.

The Twentieth Century

Nebraskans had long been inventive when it came to coaxing a living out of the often harsh landscape. New techniques had been developed for irrigating, or watering, the dry soil. To help the state along, Congress passed the Reclamation Act in 1902. It created funds to encourage and improve irrigation systems, such as the North Platte Project, which helped irrigate 165,000 acres (66,773 ha) of Nebraskan land. In the Panhandle, where farming could be especially challenging, new crops were able to thrive. Sugar beets, alfalfa, and winter wheat are major crops still grown in the state today.

In central and western Nebraska, farmers and ranchers had often clashed. Ranchers often resented the presence of farmers, who claimed land the ranchers felt could be better used for raising cattle. With Congress's passage of the Kinkaid Act, though, the farmers scored a victory. It allowed farmers to increase their holdings up to 640 acres (259 ha) and thus have a greater chance to make

Massive erosion only added to the tragedies brought by the Great Depression. A lone farmer looks on in disbelief at his dry, eroding land in Richardson County.

a success of their ventures. As a result of the act, the Sandhills saw greater development. Though many found the area too harsh to farm successfully, their efforts still helped build the area's economy. While the Sandhills did not lend themselves easily to farming, it was ideal cattle country. Ranchers bought the failed farms and expanded their holdings in the area. They fattened their herds on the grassland.

In 1917, World War I brought great change to the nation, especially Nebraska. While many brave Cornhuskers were off fighting in Europe, the state's economy boomed. There was a great demand for the wealth of farm products Nebraska produced. With the end of the war in 1919, though, the economy slumped once again. Then in 1929 came the ultimate blow. The Great Depression gripped the country and eventually the world. Jobs were scarce, people were out of work, and there was little relief in sight. The price of farm products dipped even further. Yet another drought only made matters worse. Farmers lost their land. Relief in the form of long-term, low-interest loans provided some help, but the lean years left few Nebraskans untouched.

Nebraskans were not without hope, though. The coming of World War II in 1941 brought a much-needed boost to the state's economy. Farm products were again in high demand, including cattle, oats, wheat, potatoes, and corn. The state's growing number of factories turned out war supplies. More than 128,000 Nebraskans joined the war effort, many of them fighting on the battlefields of Europe and Asia.

In the last half of the twentieth century, the state's economy changed rapidly. Still a major agricultural state, the state's farms have become larger, but fewer in number. The size of the average farm almost doubled between 1950 and the late 1990s. There are only half the number of farms there were by the end of World War II, though. Advances in technology and farm machinery have meant these larger operations require fewer workers. Many Nebraskans have needed to look for new ways of earning a living. Some have turned to the state's cities and towns as important sources of income. During the 1960s, state leaders were able to attract new businesses, mostly in manufacturing, to the state.

As the state grew, residents began moving to the state's cities and suburban areas. Today Omaha, seen here, is the forty-second largest city in the United States.

As the state's economy and centers of population shifted, new challenges arose. Once a mostly rural state, Nebraskans were faced, more and more, with problems often associated with larger cities, such as crime, urban poverty, and racial unrest. The 1960s were a period of radical change for Nebraska's African-American residents. Civil rights demonstrations, which were held to call attention to racial inequality, took place in Omaha in 1963. Then, in 1968 and 1969, race riots in that city required the US military and the National Guard to step in.

Meanwhile, in rural Nebraska, farmers faced challenges of their own. Farming became too expensive for some because there was little profit to show for the hours of labor required. Many families sold their farms and turned to another way of life. By 1970 more than 60 percent of the state's residents lived in Nebraska's cities and towns. The times marked a major shift away from rural life. The change made Nebraskans aware of the need to build industries and to draw new businesses to the state.

In the twenty-first century, many residents look to the future with confidence. They also continue to honor their roots and the times of struggle and triumph that have made the state the strong, united place it is today.

★ **1541** Spanish explorer Francisco Vásquez de Coronado leads an expedition and claims the region for Spain.

★ **1682** French explorer Sieur de La Salle claims the lands drained by the Mississippi River, including present-day Nebraska, for France.

★ **1714** Étienne Veniard de Bourgmont becomes the first recorded European to enter the area now known as Nebraska.

★ **1739** While trying to find the way to Santa Fe, Frenchmen Pierre and Paul Mallet become lost and are the first Europeans known to cross Nebraska.

★ **1803** With the Louisiana Purchase, the United States gains possession of Nebraska.

★ **1806** Explorer Zebulon Pike enters southern Nebraska.

★ **1819** Fort Atkinson, the US Army's first post in Nebraska, is built.

★ **1823** Traders and others found Bellevue, the state's first permanent settlement.

★ **1840s** Thousands of travelers along the Oregon Trail pass through the Platte River valley and past Fort Kearny.

★ **1854** Congress passes the Kansas-Nebraska Act, allowing the territories to decide whether or not slavery will be allowed within their borders.

★ **1862** The Homestead Act further opens the territory to settlement.

★ **1867** Nebraska joins the Union as the thirty-seventh state.

★ **1877** Oglala Sioux leader Crazy Horse surrenders in Nebraska.

★ **1904** The Kinkaid Act promotes settlement in the Sandhills and Panhandle.

★ **1929** The Great Depression begins, affecting residents in Nebraska and across the country.

★ **1968–1969** Race riots erupt in Omaha, prompting the arrival of the National Guard.

★ **1982** A new state law bars farmers from selling their land to corporations.

★ **2003** Nebraska celebrates the Lewis & Clark Bicentennial Commemoration.

★ **2012** The Keystone Pipeline, a proposed oil line, is rerouted away from the Sandhills after opposition from state residents.

The People

Nebraskans have always been a diverse group. The state's first residents were the Native Americans who settled in the open grasslands. Other newcomers arrived as slaves, while still more came from Europe in search of a better life. Today Nebraskans trace their roots to a variety of sources. Many come from families who have lived in the state for many generations.

Through the years, people of varying backgrounds have called the state home. Starting in the 1800s, waves of immigrants began spreading across the plains. The largest ethnic groups represented in the state today trace their roots back to Germany, Ireland, England, Sweden, and the Czech and Slovak republics. But these groups are just one part of the changing face of Nebraska in the twenty-first century. Today people from across the United States and around the world are drawn to life in the Cornhusker State. Together, they form a varied and vibrant society.

A costumed reenactor describes life on the Oregon Trail to a group of children. Nebraska's rich past has helped shape the diverse range of people who call the state home today.

Native Nebraska

Nebraska was once home to a long list of Native American groups. The Arapaho, Cheyenne, Dakota Sioux, Santee Sioux, Fox, Omaha, Oto, Pawnee, Potawatome, Ponca, and Sac are some of the major groups that made their home on the state's grasslands. These various nations once had more than 40,000 combined members. Through the years, though, their numbers declined. By the early 1910s, less than 5,000 Native Americans remained in the state. Most had been forced to move onto reservations in nearby states.

Today, more than 20,000 Native Americans call Nebraska home. They are spread across the state in cities and towns. They also live on Nebraska's three reservations—the Santee Sioux, Winnebago, and Omaha. A small group of Sac and Fox can be found living in homes on the southeastern portion of the state.

Each year, usually in July, the Winnebago Reservation hosts a two-day homecoming gathering. Councils are held, and ancient traditions revived and shared. The Santee Sioux and the Omaha also come together and hold

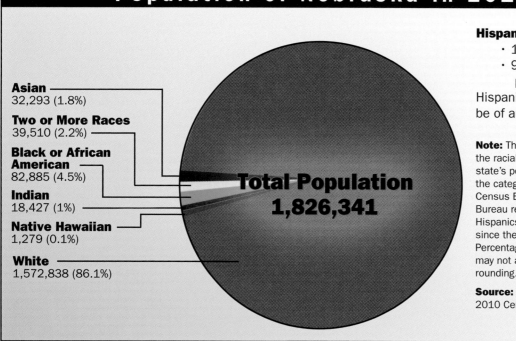

Population of Nebraska in 2010

Asian
32,293 (1.8%)

Two or More Races
39,510 (2.2%)

Black or African American
82,885 (4.5%)

Indian
18,427 (1%)

Native Hawaiian
1,279 (0.1%)

White
1,572,838 (86.1%)

**Total Population
1,826,341**

Hispanics or Latinos:
- 167,405 people
- 9.2% of the state's population

Hispanics or Latinos may be of any race.

Note: The pie chart shows the racial breakdown of the state's population based on the categories used by the US Census Bureau. The Census Bureau reports information for Hispanics or Latinos separately, since they may be of any race. Percentages in the pie chart may not add to 100 because of rounding.

Source: US Census Bureau, 2010 Census

A powwow marks a special time for Native people to come together and celebrate the dances and rituals that make their culture unique.

celebrations each summer. The events feature a variety of activities. Symbolic dances and traditional songs are performed, bringing the native past vividly to life. There is also storytelling during which native history and lore are shared and passed on. Most of all, these celebrations are a time for Nebraska's native residents to come together, visit with friends and relatives, and celebrate the bond they all share.

Czechs on the Plains

Czechs played a major role in the settling of the Cornhusker State. By 1910, 14 percent of Nebraska's foreign-born residents had come from Czechoslovakia, the largest Czech population in any US state. Crop failures and a weak economy first drove many Czechs from their homeland in the 1870s and 1880s. Many would face similar problems in their new nation. Railroad advertisements—as well as glowing articles in Czech magazines and newspapers—convinced thousands to uproot their lives and try their fortune in the paradise of the American plains. Friends and relatives were a strong draw as well. Their letters and reports home spoke of the pleasures of life on the plains.

The newly arrived Czechs were mostly farmers, but merchants and laborers came, too. Many early settlements were mostly all-Czech villages. Most immigrants chose to settle together, preferring the comfort and support of their fellow countrymen to ease the transition to life in America. From the mid-1850s until World War I, Nebraska was the top destination for Czechs coming to the United States. As was the case with many plains states at the end of the 1800s, the 1870 census revealed that nearly 25 percent of Nebraskans were foreign born.

Today many Nebraskans celebrate their Czech heritage in a variety of ways. Festivals and annual events bring the culture to life. Wilber, sometimes called the "Czech Capital of America," draws people from the across the Midwest and beyond. Recently, greater efforts have been made to honor and preserve the history of Czech life on the plains. The Czech Heritage Project is leading the way. Working with groups at the University of Nebraska, project workers are creating an archive, or collection, of photographs and letters that capture elements of early Czech-American life. The collection is available on the Internet for researchers and the public to view. A major part of the project involves translating cassette recordings made in the 1970s by state residents. Mostly told in the Czech language, these oral histories, as they are called, tell of life on the American plains. They are a key part of preserving Nebraska's rich Czech history. Some tell stories of coming to the United States and settling into mostly Czech communities where children often learned in the Czech language.

These revelers, wearing traditional clothing, perform traditional Czech dances in Wilber.

To keep close ties between the United States and the Czech Republic, the University of Nebraska-Lincoln has set up the Paul Robitschek Czech Study Program. It offers scholarships to students living in the Czech Republic. Through the program, they are given the chance to further their studies in the United States and to learn about the place many Czech people immigrated to in the 1800s and 1900s.

Famous Nebraskans

Willa Cather: Author

As a little girl, Cather and her family relocated to a barren stretch of the Nebraska plains. Though she experienced a difficult and lonely childhood, she eventually grew to love living on the prairie. Her experiences would eventually fuel her talents as a writer. In such classics as *O Pioneers!*, *My Antonia*, and *The Song of the Lark*, she captured the joys and struggles of life in the Midwest.

Gerald Ford: US President

Born in Omaha in 1913 and raised in Michigan, Gerald Ford became US president in 1974 after the resignation of the previous president, Richard Nixon. A lieutenant commander in the Navy during World War II, he was elected to Congress in 1948. As president, he attempted to address problems with the nation's economy. On the foreign front, he guided America's relations with the Soviet Union, the Middle East, and Southeast Asia.

Warren Buffett: Businessman and Philanthropist

Warren Buffett was born in Omaha in 1930 and has often been called the "Oracle of Omaha" for his talent and skill in business and financial investing. Today, he is one of the richest people in the world, with a net worth of nearly $60 billion. However, he is also one of the world's great philanthropists, and has vowed to give 99 percent of his money away to charity.

Buffalo Bill Cody: Entertainer

This colorful character arrived in Nebraska Territory as an eight-year-old boy. By fourteen, he was a rider for the Pony Express. A talented hunter, Cody earned his nickname hunting buffalo on the plains. His skills as a marksman and entertainer gave rise to his famed Wild West shows, which were presented to eager audiences in America and Europe for three decades.

Red Cloud: Warrior and Statesman

Also known as Makhpiya-Luta, Red Cloud was born near North Platte. He was schooled from an early age in the art of war, eventually rising to a position of power in the Lakota nation for his handling of territorial battles with the Crow, Pawnee, Ute, and Shoshone. In 1866 Red Cloud directed a successful war against the US government, securing peace for a number of years through the Fort Laramie Treaty. He dedicated the rest of his life to resisting the advance of settlers. He also fought against US officials who unfairly seized and distributed native-held lands. Red Cloud died in 1909.

Malcolm X: African-American Leader

In 1925, Malcolm Little was born in Omaha. In his twenties, he embraced the teachings of the Nation of Islam and changed his last name to X to reflect the loss of his true family name when his ancestors were first enslaved. Malcolm X worked to shed light on the racial abuses practiced by many whites, and he was known for his controversial speeches. Malcolm X was murdered in New York City in 1965.

African Americans

African Americans have long been a part of the history of the Cornhusker State. The first census of the territory, taken in 1854, listed only four slaves. Up until the Civil War, fewer than 100 African Americans called the state home. When the war ended—and slavery along with it—this trend changed. Slowly, African Americans began turning to the west as a place to pursue their newfound freedom.

Groups of black settlers soon began pushing into the heart of the plains. Called Exodusters, some came to Nebraska after settling in Kansas for a while. They eventually set down roots in Lincoln, Omaha, and Nebraska City. While many worked for the railroads, others lived mostly in Custer, Dawson, and Harlan counties. An all-black community was founded at Overton in 1885. More black towns, including Brownlee and DeWitty, formed in the early 1900s in Cherry County. With its large amounts of unclaimed land, western Nebraska became a draw for many black families.

The early decades of the 1900s also marked the great migration to the North. More than 500,000 blacks left their homes in the South and headed north and west. Omaha saw the greatest change. Between 1910 and 1920, its black population doubled from around 5,000 to 10,315. Its population has

Nebraska's bustling cities—such as Omaha—have become vibrant centers for the rich cultural diversity the state has to offer.

grown ever since. For many African Americans living in the state, life was not always easy. Racial tensions, killings, and riots marred the lives of many.

Through it all, the state's African-American community has stayed strong. Black Nebraskans still honor the struggles of the past, as they look to the future. Today in Nebraska's schools the state's African-American heritage is celebrated. As countless students now learn, the history of their state cannot be told without the inclusion of the African-American experience.

New Faces

As is the case in most other states, Hispanics are Nebraska's fastest-growing group. Their numbers nearly doubled during the 1990s. The state's urban areas saw the greatest jump. Douglas County, in particular, which contains the city of Omaha, was the site of the largest rise.

Asian Americans have also grown in numbers. Though a smaller presence in Nebraska overall, the state's Asian community has experienced a major population jump. During the 1990s, it grew by nearly 73 percent. Between 2000 and 2010, it grew by another 10,000 people. These figures show the broad appeal of the Cornhusker State.

Hispanics are a fast-growing group in the Cornhusker State. With her ruffles flying, this young woman performs a traditional Mexican dance.

With new industries and the rising cost of farming, parts of the rural Midwest are suffering from a population drain, as people move elsewhere in search of better opportunities. A once-thriving community, Orella, seen here, is now a ghost town being slowly reclaimed by the prairie.

People from all backgrounds are drawn to the state's peaceful communities, low crime, and strong schools. Nebraska is also an affordable place to live and raise a family. Slowly, Nebraskans are seeing their communities grow and change. While the state is still mostly white, today Nebraska sports its own vibrant blend of peoples and cultures.

The Rural Life

For centuries, Nebraska was a rural wonderland. Images of the plains and hearty pioneers making houses out of sod are a key part of the state's history. In recent years, however, the state has witnessed a major shift. More and more Nebraskans have moved to urban and suburban centers to build their lives. As farms became larger and required fewer workers, small rural towns struggled to offer other well-paying jobs.

Slowly, communities became drained of their populations. People left in search of better-paying jobs elsewhere. It is a trend occurring across most of the Great Plains. The region has lost more than two-thirds of its population since the 1920s. Once-thriving communities are now practically boarded up, just one step away from becoming ghost towns.

Many Nebraskans trace their roots to the land. The rolling plains gave rise to a state that residents now cherish and work hard to improve.

Many Nebraskans are trying to find ways to prevent this from happening. One example is the town of Superior in southern Nebraska. The people of Superior know the hardship of losing factories and businesses and the important jobs they provide. So they have joined together, creating an economic development corporation. The goals of the corporation include attracting new businesses to the town and improving existing buildings. Some are hopeful these efforts will lead to a new life for the community.

For now, most residents know that the times have changed and that their town must change with them. There are no easy solutions. In the meantime, like the people of many of the state's other rural towns, they are trying to come up with ways of coaxing tourists and new businesses to spend and invest money in their town. Still, for many of the people who stay in Nebraska's shrinking towns, the hard times have done little to lessen their love of the rural life. To them, this is the Nebraska they have always known and will always cherish.

★ Buffalo Commons Storytelling Festival

Top storytellers and musicians from across the state and the country gather each year in McCook. Cowboy poetry and ghost stories are just part of the fun at this event held around Memorial Day.

★ Nebraskaland Days

The people of North Platte welcome folk from all around to their annual June festival featuring beauty contests, sports tournaments, parades, concerts, rodeos, arts and crafts, and all the food one can eat.

★ Cottonwood Market Days

This outdoor event, called the Cottonwood Festival until 2013, is held in Hastings in the fall. It features the work of painters, sculptors, glassblowers, and jewelry makers, as well as musical performances, food, and a classic car show.

★ Oregon Trail Days

Each July, the town of Gering hosts this top frontier festival, the longest continuously running festival in Nebraska. Visitors enjoy cook-offs, square dancing, an art show, and one of the state's largest parades. For athletes, the event also features a bike race to the top of Scotts Bluff National Monument and a 5-mile (8 km) run.

★ Wayne Chicken Show

This fun event is held each July in Wayne. It features a parade, a hot wing eating contest, and plenty of chicken-themed arts and crafts. A "Cutest Chicklette" contest is held for children age four and under.

★ Germanfest

This summer event, held in Syracuse, celebrates the German heritage of many Nebraska residents. A dog race, called the "Viener Race," is held along with "Viener Vogue," a dog fashion show. There are also parades, crafts, food, and a golf tournament.

★ John C. Fremont Days

The people of Fremont gather together in July to celebrate the man who gave their town its name. Dancing, car shows, a reenactment of a frontier camp, and a talent show help to make this tribute complete.

★ Meadowlark Music Festival

Held in Lincoln, this festival celebrates classical music with a series of family-friendly performances. The festival is a great way for people from all backgrounds to experience classical music, and musicians often perform for free at schools and community centers.

How the Government Works

When it comes to their politics, Nebraskans are truly unique. They are the only people served by a state legislature that is unicameral. That means the legislature that makes state laws is made up of a single chamber, or house. Most states have two-part legislatures, made up of a senate and a house of representatives. For 68 years, Nebraska followed this pattern as well. Then, in 1934, US Senator George W. Norris proposed a change. The idea of switching to a unicameral system was first suggested in 1915, but at that time it was struck down. Some felt it was not a good idea, but it was still debated and discussed in Nebraska for almost two decades. Norris helped to finally end the years of indecision. He proposed an amendment, or change, to the state constitution calling for the creation of the unicameral system.

Those in favor of the plan believed it would make the lawmaking process simpler and more open to the public. They also argued that having a one-house system would save time and money. The new system would also change the way senators were elected. Candidates would

Quick Facts

On the federal level, Nebraska elects two people to serve in the US Senate and three people to serve in the US House of Representatives.

Nebraska's capitol building, in Lincoln, was completed in 1932 and is the tallest building in the city.

Part of the state's budget is spent on police officers and firefighters. Lawmakers must decide how much money is needed to keep important programs and services running.

not run as part of any official political party—such as Democrat or Republican. They would be judged as individuals and not as members of a larger political group. Voters would decide based on the strength of a candidate's ideas and record of service.

The voters were given the final say. In November 1934, they voted to adopt the change. The new unicameral legislature first met three years later in 1937. Norris's predictions turned out to be right. In the unicameral legislature's first year, legislative costs were chopped in half. The state's lawmakers and citizens were convinced they had made the right decision. The change shows the state was not afraid to take a bold step to fit its own unique needs.

All Kinds of Leaders

State officials are handed the tough task of running Nebraska. They create budgets and then decide how the state will spend its money on a variety of projects and programs. They also create the laws all Nebraskans must follow. These laws decide how fast you can drive on the state's roads and highways, how

Branches of Government

EXECUTIVE ★ ★ ★ ★ ★ ★ ★ ★

The governor is the head of the executive branch. He or she prepares the state budget and signs the laws that will best serve the state. A variety of other officials assist the governor. These include the lieutenant governor, secretary of state, attorney general, state treasurer, and auditor of public accounts. Each of these important positions, including the governor, is decided in a general election and carries a four-year term.

LEGISLATIVE ★ ★ ★ ★ ★ ★ ★ ★

Nebraska is the only state with a unicameral system of government. That means the state legislature is made up of a single governing body, not two like the US federal government and the other 49 states. Nebraska's legislature is made up of 49 voting members who do not identify or associate themselves with any specific political party. They each serve terms of four years.

JUDICIAL ★ ★ ★ ★ ★ ★ ★ ★

The supreme court is the state's highest judicial body. The governor chooses the chief justice while the six other judges are selected from each of six districts in the state and serve six-year terms. The state is also served by lesser courts, including courts of appeals, twelve district courts, and courts that hear cases in each of the state's counties.

many days children go to school, and many other issues important to the daily lives of Nebraska's citizens. In a state with so many people, Nebraska's officials try to address the needs and concerns of all.

Most Nebraskans do not need to serve in the capitol in Lincoln in order to make a difference. There is plenty to be done in their own counties and communities. Nebraska's cities and towns are grouped together to form 93 counties. About two-thirds of these counties are run by a board of commissioners. Each board is typically made up of three to five members. Other counties are led by a seven-member board of supervisors. Board members oversee almost all aspects of county business. A variety of people help the board members in carrying out their duties. Clerks, treasurers, lawyers, police officers, and school superintendents are just some of the people who work hard to improve life in Nebraska's counties.

At a more local level, voters choose mayors or boards of commissioners to oversee the daily affairs in Nebraska's many cities, towns, and communities. These public servants play many different roles. They serve as lawmakers and managers. With more than 500 cities, towns, and villages, it takes a lot of people to make life in Nebraska run smoothly. They make sure the state's citizens have access to government-run services and programs. They also approve the funds for such important tasks as building and improving roads and buying new books for public libraries.

From Bill to Law

A bill is an idea for a new law. It can also suggest ways of changing laws that already exist. Bills are first introduced by a sponsor, usually a state senator. Sometimes the ideas for laws come straight from ordinary citizens.

Once the senator has presented the bill, it is given a number by the clerk. The title of the bill is then read to the members of the legislature, after which it is sent to the reference committee. This is a group of nine senators who together form the executive board. They will move the bill along to what is known as a standing committee, a group of senators who will look more closely into the issues surrounding the bill. At the same time, the bill is published. Copies are made available to all senators as well as to the general public.

When the standing committee meets to discuss the bill, it holds a public hearing. This important step means the state senators hear from a variety of citizens. It gives Nebraskans a chance to come and express their opinions on issues that are important to them.

If the standing committee approves of the bill, it then goes to what is known as the general file. This is a daily list of bills the senators will be discussing and voting on. They consider all parts of the bill, including any amendments, or changes, the standing committee has made. Then it comes time to vote. If at least twenty-five state senators are in favor of the bill, it is reviewed to be sure it is in its proper form.

More changes can come at any time, which the legislature, again, must approve. The bill is then in its final form. Copies are once again sent to the senators. After the senators have read the entire bill, they take the final vote. If the bill is approved, it is sent to the governor. The governor can sign the bill and make it an official part of state law. He or she can also veto, or reject, the bill. If this happens, three-fifths, or at least thirty members, of the state legislature must still be in favor of the measure for it to become law. Once approved, the bill goes into effect in three months' time. It is then an official part of Nebraska state law.

Contacting Lawmakers

★ ★ ★ ★ ★ ★ ★ ★ ★ ★ ★ ★

If you are interested in contacting Nebraska's state legislators, go to

http://nebraskalegislature.gov/senators

You can search for legislators and their contact information by name, zip code, or district.

Dave Heineman became Nebraska's governor in 2005 when the previous governor resigned. He was then elected to the office in 2006 and 2010.

Making a Living

Nebraska's greatest resources are its rich soils and plentiful water. Hardworking farmers have built Nebraska into one of the nation's leading farming states. The state's success has always been built on its crops and cattle. Through the twentieth century, the state's farms have changed, though. Fewer people now make a living directly from the land. The state's citizens have often been forced to change the way they make a living. New industries have emerged in the Cornhusker State. They offer Nebraskans different choices in the careers they pursue. While large combines and grain elevators are still a common sight in the state, so are businesses and factories that produce and sell a wide range of products.

Agriculture

From meat to beans to grains, many Nebraska products end up on America's dinner tables every day. Farming is not always an easy venture in the Cornhusker State, though. To encourage strong harvests, farmers have adopted a variety of methods that save soil and water. They have led the way in the use of irrigation, crop rotation, and dry farming. Dry farming is a method used in very dry places. Crops that are resistant to drought are planted so there is no need for irrigation.

A variety of Nebraska wildlife is featured in this popular display at Cabela's in Sidney. The outdoor-supply store has added much to the state's wealth, providing many jobs and drawing shoppers and browsers from all around.

Nebraska's Industries and Workers (May 2013)

Industry	Number of People Working in That Industry	Percentage of Labor Force Working in That Industry
Farming	29,800	3%
Mining, Logging, and Construction	42,700	4.2%
Manufacturing	97,300	9.7%
Trade, Transportation, and Utilities	199,400	20%
Information	17,000	1.7%
Financial Activities	72,500	7.2%
Professional & Business Services	106,700	10.7%
Education & Health Services	142,500	14.2%
Leisure & Hospitality	84,200	8.4%
Other Services	37,000	3.7%
Government	169,000	16.9%
Totals	**998,100**	**99.7%**

Notes: Figures above do not include people in the armed forces. "Professionals" includes people such as doctors and lawyers.

Source: U.S. Bureau of Labor Statistics

The state's major crops include corn, soybeans, dry beans, wheat, hay, grain sorghum, potatoes, and sugar beets. Grapes, tomatoes, and orchard fruits are also grown from the land. The southwestern plateau is wheat country.

Sugar beets and dry edible beans are another top crop grown there as well as in parts of the Panhandle. The state currently leads the nation in the production of great northern beans and produces about 11 percent of all dry beans grown in the United States. In parts of the state where the soil is loose and sandy, many farmers have had success planting potatoes.

Currently 8.2 million acres (3.3 million ha) of Nebraska farmland benefit from irrigation. The many dams built on the state's 24,000 miles (38,624 km) of rivers and streams have helped this system become a success.

RECIPE FOR CHOCOLATE-COVERED POPCORN BALLS

Corn is an important crop on many Nebraska farms. Use this recipe to make a sweet treat out of tasty popcorn.

WHAT YOU NEED

8 cups of popcorn (popped and ready to eat)

1/2 cup granulated sugar

1/2 cup corn syrup

1/4 cup butter or margarine

2 tablespoons cocoa powder (unsweetened)

1/2 cup chopped peanuts

1 cup mini-marshmallows

Have an adult help you combine the sugar, corn syrup, butter, and cocoa in a medium-sized pan. Carefully stir these ingredients over a low heat on the stove and bring the mixture slowly to a boil. Make sure the ingredients do not get too hot or they will stick to the bottom of the pan. Once bubbles appear, turn off the heat and remove the pan from the stove. All the ingredients in the pan should be melted and look like a slightly gooey sauce.

Next, have an adult help you pour this mixture over the popcorn. One person can pour the sauce while the other person stirs the popcorn. Add the peanuts and the marshmallows and stir again until everything is coated in the chocolate sauce.

Wait until this mixture has cooled enough so that it will not burn your hands. Wash your hands, coat your fingers with some butter, and shape the chocolate popcorn mixture into balls about the size of tennis balls.

Let the popcorn balls cool and then enjoy! NOTE: This recipe makes about 18 popcorn balls.

Cattle are raised in all of Nebraska's 93 counties. The Sandhills, in particular, are prime cattle country. Herds of Angus and Hereford cattle spend the spring and summer feasting on the abundant grasses. Nebraska currently leads the nation in the production of red meat. Though less valuable to the state's economy, hogs, dairy cattle, sheep, and chickens are raised as well. These operations are mostly found in the eastern part of the state, which supports a more diverse economy.

Mineral Wealth

Nebraska is not known for its mining industry. Still, plenty of mineral wealth lies locked beneath its soils. Oil and natural gas are found in the Panhandle, mostly in Kimball and Cheyenne counties. Oil was first discovered in the state in 1939. By the early 1940s, several companies had begun drilling, and in no time, oil had become the state's most valuable mineral resource.

Sand and gravel are major state products as well. Large quantities are gathered from across the state, but mostly along the Republican and Platte river valleys. Once collected, they are used mostly in concrete and for the surfaces of roads.

A worker in Omaha inspects a model for a proposed oil refinery.

In an Omaha laboratory, two technicians study seedlings in an attempt to learn how the state's fields and farms can become more productive.

Similarly, stone is plentiful in the state, mostly in the southern and eastern regions. Limestone, sandstone, chalkrock, and smaller amounts of quartzite are also used in road building and in the creation of cement. Limestone quarries are found along the Missouri River in the state's southeastern stretch. Clay, needed mostly in making tiles and bricks, is another treasure offered up from the Nebraska countryside. It is found across the state and is a major part of the soil of the badlands.

Manufacturing, Services, and Retail

Nebraskans make and manufacture a variety of items. Clocks, magnets, furniture, fans, golf clubs, and pipe organs are just some of the things produced in the state. Workers also produce large-scale items in some of the state's major factories. The creation of machinery, farm equipment, and car parts helps keep people working and on the go. The state's farmers need to be able to plant and harvest their crops. Truck drivers, too, must be able to transport farm products to processing centers across the state. It is not surprising, then, that a successful industry has emerged in the state by supplying workers with these items.

Since Nebraska is such a major agricultural state, food processing is also big business. Currently the processing and creation of food products is the state's largest source of income. Dairy items, meats, and flour and flour-based products such as cereals and pasta are just some of the foods that are prepared in the Cornhusker State. Workers also process grain to feed to the state's large herds of livestock.

These various business operations can be found across the state. The state's largest economic center, though, is Omaha. Slowly through the years, the city has emerged as a major business center. Food processing, insurance,

Hereford cattle, seen here, originated in England and were brought to the United States in 1817.

Sorghum

Sorghum is one of the state's main grain crops, grown mostly in the southeastern and south-central portions. It is used mostly as feed for cattle, hogs, and chickens. It is well-suited to the Nebraska climate and is able to thrive in areas with high heat and little water. The head of the plant sports hundreds of "berries" and can be red, white, bronze, or yellowish.

Machinery and Transportation Equipment

Farmers and ranchers need a lot of equipment—tractors, grain elevators, and combines, just to name a few. Nebraska's workers also produce equipment for tractor trailers, trucks, and other giants of the road.

Corn

Corn is the most widely grown crop in the state, with about 10 million acres (404,686 ha) used for its production. Corn is used to feed livestock and poultry and produce ethanol, which can be used as a fuel. Corn can even be made into a type of plastic.

Dry Edible Beans

Nebraska is the country's third-largest producer of these tiny legumes. Kidney beans, great northern beans, and pinto beans help to keep the nation—and the world—well fed.

Cattle and Calves

Nebraska has more than 23 million acres (9,307,000 ha) of range and pastureland, about half of which is in the Sandhills. This vast amount of land has helped the state become the leading producer of red meat in the country, with more than 7 billion pounds (3.17 billion kg) of meat from cows produced in 2011. Other cows are raised for their milk to make dairy products, which are also big business in the state.

Wheat

Nebraska produces hard red winter wheat and hard white winter wheat, which are used in many types of breads and pastas. Wheat production in the state is valued at over $300 million each year, and about half of the wheat grown in Nebraska is sent to other countries.

Nature lovers gather along the boardwalk at Indian Cave State Park. Tourism is a major money earner for the Cornhusker State.

telecommunications, and health care are just some of the major industries that keep residents of Omaha busy.

Lincoln is another business center. In addition to the University of Nebraska, which employs thousands of people, the state capital hosts a wealth of companies that produce medicine and related medical products, transportation parts and equipment, and many other things. Insurance and telecommunications are important Lincoln industries as well.

It takes a wide range of Nebraskans to keep the state productive and strong. Doctors, mechanics, cooks, librarians, and real estate agents are just some of the many roles state residents fill in order to serve and assist their fellow Nebraskans. To many of the state's citizens, the pioneer spirit is still alive, and helping each other out is not an old-fashioned notion. Though the state has changed a lot since the days Native Americans freely roamed the plains, Nebraskans know that whatever challenges the future brings, they will face them together.

Nebraska was one of the last states to adopt its own official flag. In 1925, lawmakers set out to change that, adopting a banner that consisted of "a reproduction of the Great Seal of the State charged on the center in gold and silver on a field of national blue." Although it was technically adopted in that year, at the time this important symbol was called the state banner and not named Nebraska's official flag until 1965.

In 1867, one of the bills lawmakers adopted called for the creation of the state seal. It would show "a steamboat ascending the Missouri River, the mechanic arts . . . represented by a smith with a hammer and anvil, in the foreground, agriculture to be represented by a settlers cabin, sheaves of wheat, and stalks of growing corn, in the background a train of cars heading towards the Rocky Mountains, and on the extreme west, the Rocky Mountains to be plainly in view [and] around the top of the circle, to be in capital letters, the motto: 'Equality Before the Law.'" Finally, circling the seal are the words "Great Seal of the State of Nebraska March 1, 1867."

Nebraska State Map

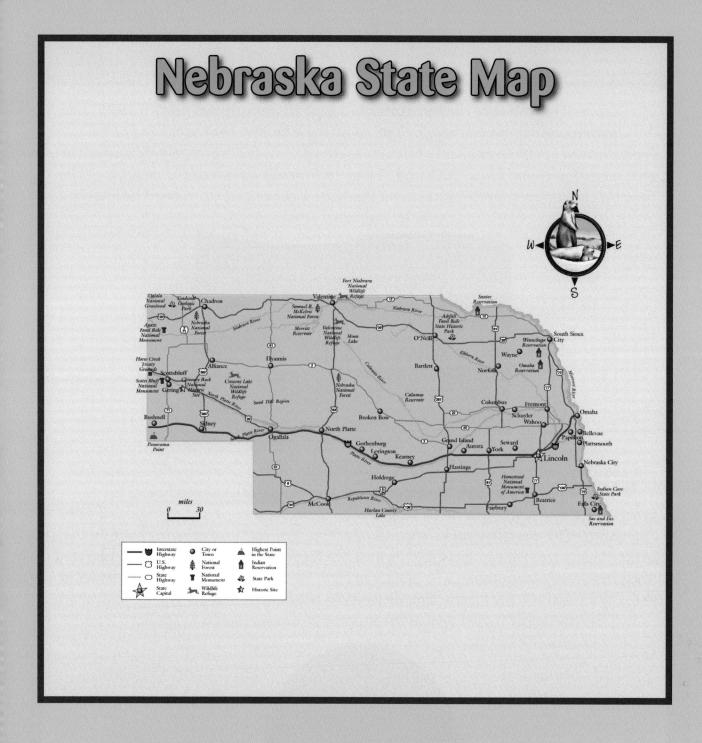

Beautiful Nebraska

words by James Fras and Guy Gage Miller
music by James Fras

Beau-ti-ful Ne-bra-ska, peace-ful prai-rie land. Laced with ma-ny ri-vers

and the hills of sand: Dark green val-leys cra-dled in the earth. Rain and sun-shine

bring a-bun-dant birth. Beau-ti-ful Ne-bra-ska, as you look a-round, You will find a rain-bow

reach-ing to the ground: All these won-ders by the Mas-ter's hand: Beau-ti-ful Ne-bra-ska

land. We are so proud of this state where we

live. There is no place that has so much to give.

Beau-ti-ful Ne-bra-ska, as you look a-round, you will find a rain-bow reach-ing to the ground:

All these won-ders by the Mas-ter's hand. Beau-ti-ful Ne-bra-ska land.

BOOKS

Monnig, Alex. *Nebraska Cornhuskers*. Inside College Football. Minneapolis, MN: ABDO Publishing, 2013.

Plain, Nancy. *Light on the Prairie: Solomon D. Butcher, Photographer of Nebraska's Pioneer Days*. Lincoln, NE: Bison Books, 2013.

Weatherly, Myra. *Nebraska*. From Sea to Shining Sea. Danbury, CT: Children's Press, 2009.

WEBSITES

Nebraska for Kids
http://www.visitnebraska.com/kids

Nebraska State Historical Society–Kids! Stuff
http://www.nebraskahistory.org/oversite/kidstuff

Nebraska Wildlife Federation
http://www.nebraskawildlife.org

Official Website of Nebraska
http://www.nebraska.gov

Doug Sanders lives in New York. One of his favorite vacations was spent in the Panhandle of Nebraska. Highlights included visits to Toadstool Geologic Park, Fort Robinson, and Agate Fossil Beds National Monument.